ENFIELD AND WOOD GREEN TRAMWAYS

Series editor Robert J Harley

Dave Jones

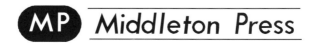

MP Middleton Press

Cover Picture: One of the finest public transport vehicles ever to serve Enfield was the Feltham type tramcar. Here London Transport car 2081, formerly Metropolitan Electric Tramways car 337, waits at the terminus of service 29 which linked Enfield with Tottenham Court Road. (W.A.Camwell)

Cover Colours: These are similar to the final livery employed by the MET.

--------- FEATURES IN LONDON *TRAMWAY CLASSICS* ---------

- **Rolling Stock**

A class. LCC	**Southwark and Deptford**
Alexandra Palace Elec. Rly.	**Enfield and Wood Green**
B class. LCC/Bexley	**Greenwich and Dartford**
B type MET	**Stamford Hill**
Barking cars	**Ilford and Barking**
Bexley cars.	**Greenwich and Dartford**
Bluebird. LCC car 1	**Camberwell and West Norwood**
C class. LCC	**Victoria and Lambeth**
Cable cars	**Clapham and Streatham**
Croydon cars	**Croydon's Tramways**
C type MET/LT	**Barnet and Finchley**
D class. LCC	**Wandsworth and Battersea**
Dartford cars	**Greenwich and Dartford**
East Ham cars	**East Ham and West Ham**
Erith cars	**Greenwich and Dartford**
E class. LCC/LT	**Aldgate and Stepney**
E1 class. LCC/LT	**Lewisham and Catford**
E1 cars 552-601. LCC/LT	**Hampstead and Highgate**
E1 cars 1777 - 1851 LCC/LT	**Clapham and Streatham**
E3 class. LCC/LT	**Camberwell and West Norwood**
E3 class. Leyton/LT	**Walthamstow and Leyton**
E type MET/LT	**Enfield and Wood Green**
Experimental Tramcars MET/LUT/LT	**Barnet and Finchley**
F class. LCC	**Embankment and Waterloo**
G class. LCC	**Embankment and Waterloo**
G type MET/LT	**Stamford Hill**
Gravesend & Northfleet cars	**North Kent**
H class (works). LCC/LT	**Eltham and Woolwich**
H type MET/LT	**Stamford Hill**
Horse cars. North Met./LCC	**Aldgate and Stepney**
HR2 class. LCC/LT	**Camberwell and W Norwood**
Ilford cars	**Ilford and Barking**
L class (works). LCC/LT	**Holborn and Finsbury**
L/1 class (works) LCC/LT	**Clapham and Streatham**
Leyton cars	**Walthamstow and Leyton**
LT car 2	**Wandsworth and Battersea**
LUT car 341	**Kingston and Wimbledon**
M class. LCC/LT	**Greenwich and Dartford**
Petrol electric cars. LCC	**Southwark and Deptford**
SMET cars	**Croydon's Tramways**
T type. LUT	**Kingston and Wimbledon**
Trailer cars LCC	**Clapham and Streatham**
Walthamstow cars	**Walthamstow and Leyton**
West Ham cars	**East Ham and West Ham**

- **Miscellaneous**

Advertising on tramcars	**Aldgate and Stepney**
Conduit system	**Embankment and Waterloo**
Power supply	**Walthamstow and Leyton**
Request stops	**Victoria and Lambeth**
Section boxes	**Eltham and Woolwich**
Track layouts - single & loops	**Stamford Hill**
Track Construction and Maintenance	**Barnet and Finchley**
Tram tours	**Holborn and Finsbury**

Published November 1997

ISBN 1 901706 03 6

© *Middleton Press*

Design Deborah Goodridge

Published by
 Middleton Press
 Easebourne Lane
 Midhurst, West Sussex
 GU29 9AZ
Tel: 01730 813169
Fax: 01730 812601

Printed & bound by Biddles Ltd,
 Guildford and Kings Lynn

CONTENTS

INTRODUCTION AND ACKNOWLEDGEMENTS

I have written this book to complement my earlier volume on the tramways of Hampstead and Highgate, and I hope a further journey along streets long since congested with motor traffic will evoke some nostalgia for the past. This was a past when the tramcar supplied reliable, efficient public transport. My thanks go to all those who have made this book possible: the National Tramway Museum for the collections of W.A.Camwell, D.W.K.Jones, H.Nicol, M.J.O'Connor and H.B.Priestley; the London Transport Museum for permission to use official MET pictures, maps and timetables; the LCC Tramways Trust for use of the Don Thompson collection; Graham Dalling, Local History Of-ficer for Enfield; Terry Russell for the type E car plan; G.Bromberger, C.Carter, A.B.Cross, B.J.Cross, J.Hambley, S.G.Jackman, C.F.Klapper, Lens of Sutton, E.Masterman, A.D.Packer, J.Pullen, G.N.Southerden, R.Stevenson and J.Wills. I am also grateful to the founding editor of *Tramway Classics*, Robert Harley, for his help and advice; likewise, I am indebted to John Barrie for checking through the manuscript and contributing much information.

Readers are reminded that further, in-depth information can be obtained from the scholarly, two volume study *The Metropolitan Electric Tramways* produced by Cyril Smeeton.

GEOGRAPHICAL SETTING

Highways leading north and west from the capital cross the former County of Middlesex and the rather hilly area which now forms part of the urban sprawl of North London. Enfield has been a market town since 1303 and over the centuries isolated villages have expanded and suburban housing now covers what was once green fields. In 1965 Enfield absorbed the neighbouring boroughs of Southgate and Edmonton.

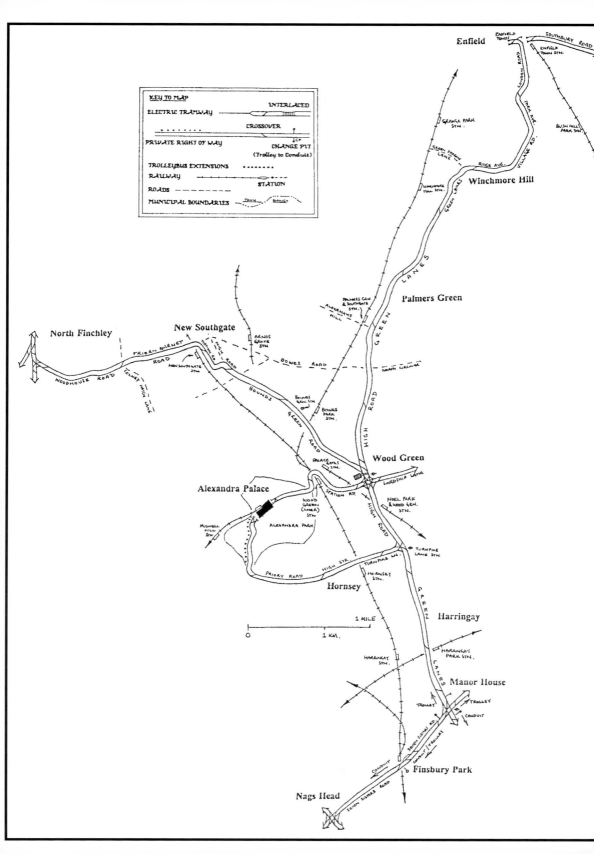

HISTORICAL BACKGROUND

Mechanical traction came to the streets of Wood Green in 1887 when on 24th December a service of steam trams was inaugurated between the Town Hall and Manor House. The operating company, the North London Tramways, soon got into financial difficulties and was sold in August 1891 to the North Metropolitan Tramways. Horse trams then replaced the defective steam vehicles, a new depot was built on Jolly Butchers Hill, and the service was extended from Manor House and Finsbury Park through Holloway and Canonbury to terminate at Moorgate. The section of track between the depot and Wood Green Town Hall was later abandoned.

At the turn of the twentieth century an alliance was forged between the Middlesex County Council and a new company, the Metropolitan Electric Tramways, with the aim of electrifying the old horse tramways and constructing new lines to the outer suburbs. Finsbury Park to Manor House, Harringay and Wood Green opened for passenger traffic on 22nd July 1904. The former horse tram depot at Wood Green had already been reconstructed for electric vehicles. New electric tracks were inaugurated in Lordship Lane as the Wood Green to Bruce Grove service opened on 20th August 1904. Meanwhile preparations had been going ahead in the Alexandra Palace area and on 6th December 1905 the Turnpike Lane to Alexandra Palace West section was joined to the MET network. Alexandra Palace East to Wood Green followed on 1!th April 1906 when a through service of single deck, type E cars, commenced between the Palace and Bruce Grove, Tottenham. Northwards from Wood Green the system began to take shape as the Ranelagh in Bounds Green Road was reached on 28th November 1906, and New Southgate Station on 11th May 1907; finally, on 8th April 1909 a connection was made via Woodhouse Road with the Finchley routes. Electric trams opened the service to Palmers Green on 6th June 1907, and the line was extended to Winchmore Hill on 1st August 1908. A new highway was constructed north of Winchmore Hill and tracks were laid to Enfield, the service opening on 1st July 1909. A futher electric tramway connection to Enfield along Southbury Road from Ponders End opened

on 20th February 1911. This line terminated outside Enfield GER Station, but due to road widening difficulties it was never connected with the main Enfield to Wood Green route.

The MET concluded through running agreements with the neighbouring London County Council and a service was started from Enfield to Euston Road on 1st August 1912. Cars on this route changed current collection at Finsbury Park from the MET's overhead wires to the LCC's conduit system. In 1912/13 route numbers began to be used throughout the LCC tramways and they were also applied to joint LCC/MET services.

Services as at July 1913:

18	Stamford Hill - Bruce Grove - Wood Green - Finsbury Park
21	North Finchley - Wood Green - Finsbury Park - Holborn
26	Enfield Town - Southbury Road - Ponders End Fire Station
28	Finsbury Park - Turnpike Lane - Muswell Hill
29	Enfield - Wood Green - Finsbury Park - Tottenham Court Road
30	The Wellington - Turnpike Lane - Alexandra Palace West
31	Palmers Green - Finsbury Park - Tottenham Court Road
32	Wood Green - Wood Green Station - Alexandra Palace East
34	Wood Green - New Southgate - North Finchley

Passenger traffic increased throughout the First World War, and after hostilities ceased the spectre of motor bus competition once again began to haunt the tramways. Various improvements were made to the rolling stock and the service was generally speeded up; only the Alexandra Palace routes remained virtually unchanged, due mainly to their unsatisfactory financial performance. The luxurious Feltham cars entered service during 1931 on local routes 21 and 29, and new loading islands were constructed at Turnpike Lane and Manor House in association with works connected with the extension of the Piccadilly Line from Finsbury Park to Arnos Grove. The new tube line opened on 19th September 1932.

Services as at June 1933:

18	*Bruce Grove Station - Lordship Lane - Wood Green (Piccadilly Line) Station*
21	*North Finchley - Wood Green - Finsbury Park - Holborn*
26	*Enfield Town - Southbury Road - Ponders End*
29	*Enfield - Wood Green - Finsbury Park - Tottenham Court Road (joint MET/LCC cars)*
32	*Wood Green (Piccadilly Line) Station - Wood Green LNER Station - Alexandra Palace East*
34	*The Wellington - Muswell Hill - Alexandra Palace West*
41	*Winchmore Hill - Wood Green - Manor House - Moorgate (LCC cars)*
51	*Muswell Hill - Manor House - Aldersgate*
71	*Aldersgate - Finsbury Park - Wood Green - Bruce Grove - Stamford Hill - Hackney - Aldgate (LCC cars)*

On 1st July 1933, control of most of London's public transport passed to the London Passenger Transport Board; very little time was lost in determining the fate of the tramways. Some route alterations were instituted by the new board, but it was soon apparent that the chosen successor to the rail bound vehicle was the electric trolleybus, and preparations were put in hand to effect the conversion. On 2nd August 1936, some of Finchley Depot's Feltham cars were transferred to Wood Green, and some months later, on 23rd February 1938, the Alexandra Palace routes were replaced by a motor bus route. Tram routes 21 and 51 perished on 6th March 1938; Wood Green's last routes to Enfield, Tottenham Court Road and Moorgate were replaced by trolleybuses on 8th May 1938. This left only route 71 from Wood Green to Aldgate and this ceased on 5th February 1939. The era of electric traction on local streets finally ended in 1961 when the trolleybuses were replaced by diesel buses.

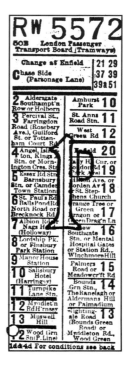

ENFIELD

1. We begin our journey not long after the Enfield tramways opened in the summer of 1909. The conductor is about to give the starting signal to the motorman and the bright vermilion and white car 78 will then move off in the direction of Wood Green and Finsbury Park. Underneath the indicator box can be seen the route symbol - a white cross on a blue background with a red letter W, denoting the Wood Green, Winchmore Hill and Enfield service. A couple of horses and carts plus a trio of bicycles are the only competing traffic.   (G.Bromberger Coll.)

Enfield 1914

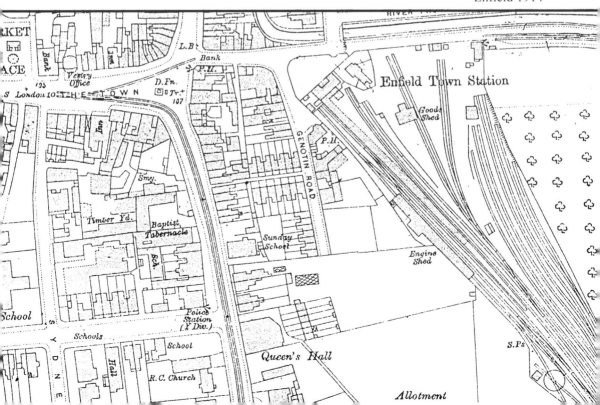

2.   We advance in time to the 1920s to observe the smartly dressed motorman in charge of car 266. This vehicle of type H (fully described in companion volume *Stamford Hill Tramways*) was later given a driver's windscreen and passed to London Transport ownership as car 2198. The frequency of the Enfield to Tottenham Court Road service was a tram every 4-6 minutes, so the photographer had better hurry up before the next car wants to use the terminus!   (J.Hambley Coll.)

3. The next visitor to the Enfield terminus is a former Walthamstow car, now in full LT red and cream livery and renumbered 2049. These faster trams started to appear in the area from September 1933 and in tandem with the Felthams they managed to maintain a respectable 58 minutes from terminus to terminus. Note the advertising on the side of the car for the famous "Shilling - All Day" facility. (G.N.Southerden)

4. Feltham car 2070 momentarily has both trolleys up as it waits in the last few months of tramways at Enfield. The trolleybus wiring presages a new era in local transportation and soon route 629 will be turning here and the Feltham will be running in South London. (R.J.Harley Coll.)

5. The date is 30th September 1932 and we view the scene from the top deck of a tram at the terminus. Note the abandoned spur rails leading towards Southbury Road; unfortunately this piece of track never connected with the other Enfield terminus outside the GER station. (H.Nicol)

6. Trams from Ponders End terminated outside Enfield Town Station, and this area is seen shortly before the service along Southbury Road was converted to buses on 16th October 1938. Views of type G cars on route 49A are very rare; normally only non-windscreen H type cars operated this service (D.A.Thompson)

7. We now look west through the town centre where car 218 is loading passengers. To the right of the tram is an automatic trolley reverser, these devices were normally only used by open top cars and they had fallen into disuse by the late 1920s. (J.Wills Coll.)

8. This postcard view is headed "Tramroad between Winchmore Hill and Bush Hill Park" (nowadays Ridge Avenue) and illustrates the new thoroughfare pioneered by the MET. This new road was open to all vehicles, not just tramcars. Note the complete absence of housing development. (G.Bromberger Coll.)

WINCHMORE HILL TO PALMERS GREEN

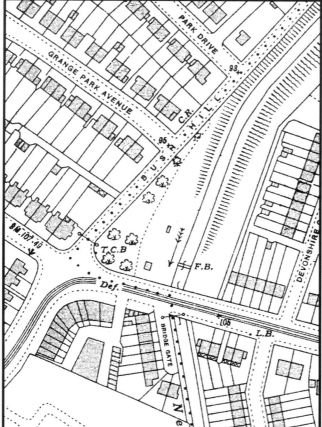

9. Car 2282, an ex-MET type C/1 car 192 (this type is featured in *Barnet and Finchley Tramways*), is at the Green Dragon Lane, Winchmore Hill terminus of route 39A. Type C/1 cars were rare vistors to this area. As the tram is displaying route 39, it is possible that the car has been diverted by an inspector to cover a gap in service to Winchmore Hill. This was a common practice in tram days, but was strictly forbidden in the bus side of London Transport. (A.D.Packer Coll.)

Winchmore Hill 1935

10. Spring blossom adorns the trees by Green Dragon Lane as the crew of car 2264 pose for a photograph before they set off back to Moorgate. Former MET cars only appeared on this route during the last two months of service, when operation was transferred from Holloway Depot to Wood Green Depot. The journey was timetabled at 48 minutes and the through fare from Manor House to Winchmore Hill was a mere three old pence - just over 1p! (W.A.Camwell)

41 MANOR HOUSE — MOORGATE
Via Green Lanes, Mildmay Park, Southgate Rd., East Rd.
Extended weekday rush hours to Winchmore Hill.
Service Int. Moorgate — Manor House 2–8 mins.
Manor House — Winch. Hill 6 mins.
Journey time Moorgate—Manor House 23 mins.
Winch. Hill 48 mins.
Through fare Moorgate—Manor House 3d
Manor House — Winch. Hill 4d.

Manor House to Moorgate	4 26	5 24	12 7		4 26	5 24	12 7		6 28	12 10	......
Moorgate to Manor House	4 57	5 50	12 32		4 57	5 50	12 30		6 51	12 35	......
Winchmore Hill to Moorgate	6 52	6 58	8 58		6 53	6 59	9 13		......	......	......
	4 43	4 49	7 31		1219	1225	3 9		......	......	......
Moorgate to Winchmore Hill	6 45	6 52	8 10		6 45	6 52	8 24				
	3 53	3 59	7 5		1127	1133	2 18				

11. Car 81 is pictured in splendid isolation at the northern end of Green Lanes, with the Green Dragon public house in the distance. The sign on the right is evidence of the continuing urban spread of the metropolis, it advertises for sale "A Residence and Park" which no doubt will be turned later into suburban housing. (A.D.Packer Coll.)

12. LCC car 1065 belongs to the standard E/1 class which was so familiar to Londoners, indeed its shape influenced tramway vehicle design in the capital for many years. Here it is seen passing the Broadway, Winchmore Hill. Note that although the tramtracks were well paved, the rest of the roadway leaves a lot to be desired, and for many cyclists and motorists it was a case of dodging the potholes. (D.Jones Coll.)

13. St.John's Church, Palmers Green shows a rather exotic mixture of architectural styles. Car 18 passes on its way to Finsbury Park in this scene dated around 1910. In front of the church is a sewer vent pipe which has been adapted to carry a signpost and street lamps; the tram stop is fixed to the traction standard behind.   (J.Hambley Coll.)

14. This view outside The Fox public house is entitled The Promenade, Palmers Green. The delivery van of Jones Bros. of Holloway seems to have purloined the tram track for a smoother ride. The motorman of car 20 keeps an eye out for intending passengers.   (D.Jones Coll.)

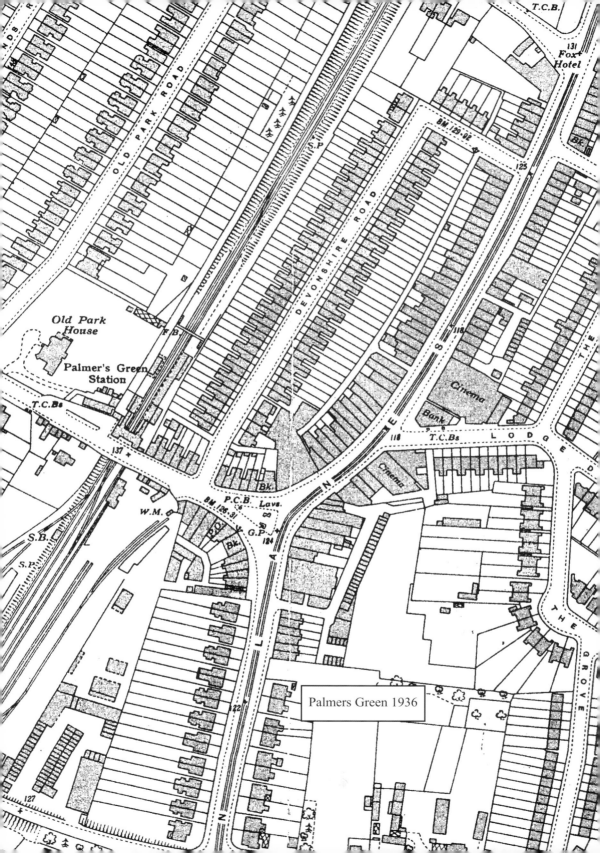

Palmers Green 1936

15. The 1920s proved somewhat of a boom time for Palmers Green as prosperity and an increase in suburban house building went hand in hand. A covered top MET tramcar glides sedately along well maintained tracks as a couple of upstart motorists scuttle away. In case you were expecting entertainment at the Paladium, Green Lanes - look again! The Palmadium sets a pun standard all of its own! (G.Bromberger Coll.)

16. Car 89 looks to be in "as delivered" condition as it makes one of the first passenger runs to Palmers Green. The date is June 1907, and the rails were extended northwards to Winchmore Hill by August of the following year. Car 89 lasted into the LT era and was eventually retired in 1936 with the fleet number 2423. (J.Hambley Coll.)

WOOD GREEN TO NEW SOUTHGATE
AND NORTH FINCHLEY

17. We now arrive at the old borough boundary of Wood Green and Southgate in the High Road near the entrance to Spencer Avenue. A bright, sunny day shows up the appalling state of the road surface, which the passengers leaving car 65 would soon have to cross.   (J.Wills Coll.)

18. In the opposite direction to the previous view we now observe car 79 bringing up the rear of a sister vehicle. Perhaps the tram in front had been delayed for some reason. Lascotts Road is on the right hand side.   (J.Wills Coll.)

19. An E/1 tram, one of the four cars of the "500" series operating at that time from Holloway Depot, proceeds across the junction of High Road with Bounds Green Road. The rails leading to New Southgate are already redundant as service 21 has succumbed to trolleybus operation. One of the new vehicles and an LT tower wagon can just be seen in the distance by the depot. Very shortly service 41 will also go the same way and the rumble of tramcars over the crossing will cease for ever.   (D.Jones Coll.)

21	NTH. FINCHLEY — WOOD GRN. — HOLBORN Via Friern Barnet Road, Bounds Green Road, Wood Green, Green Lanes, Manor House, Seven Sisters Road, Finsbury Park, Holloway, Caledonian Road, Barnsbury, Kings Cross, Grays Inn Road. Service Interval 4—5 mins. Journey time 60 mins. Through fare, 9d.		MON. to FRI.		SATURDAY		SUNDAY	
			First	Last	First	Last	First	Last
	Tally Ho Corner to Holborn.....................		5 50	5 58	10 31	5 58	6 7	10 30	7 54	10 3
	Tally Ho Corner to Finsbury Park		5 2	5 16	11 40	5 2	5 16	12 25	7 54	12 2
	Tally Ho Corner to Wood Green...............		5 2	5 16	12 50	5 2	5 16	12 50	7 54	12 5
	Wood Green to Finsbury Park..................		3 14	4 7	11 59	3 14	4 7	12 44	7 14	12 4
			......	4 35	......	......	4 35	......	......	.....
	Wood Green to Holborn..........................		3 14	4 7	10 50	3 14	4 7	10 49	7 14	10 5
			......	6 12	......	......	6 13	......	......	.....
	Holborn to Tally Ho Corner....................		4 0	4 48	11 30	4 0	4 48	11 30	7 54	11 3
			......	6 53	......	......	6 53	......	......	.....
	Holborn to Wood Green..........................		4 0	4 48	11 30	4 0	4 48	11 30	7 54	11 3
			......	6 53	......	......	6 53	......	......	.....
	Wood Green to Tally Ho Corner..............		4 37	5 4	12 29	4 37	5 4	12 30	8 30	12 3

20. The same junction as the previous view, but this time car 2074 sweeps into Bounds Green Road under the newly installed trolleybus overhead. (D.Jones Coll.)

21. The double track formation which characterised all MET routes inevitably involved expensive road widening. Here on Bounds Green Road, at the corner of Nightingale Road, car 107 slows for a tram stop.   (J.Hambley Coll.)

22. Another early view of Bounds Green Road shows car 48 passing some of the new walls and fencing erected by the contractors who also reconstructed the highway. In the foreground is a power feed to the overhead wires; by law, these were situated at half mile/750 metre intervals. (D.Jones Coll.)

→

24. The gas lamp on the left guards the entrance to New Southgate Station which was opened in August 1850. A later arrival on the scene, in May 1907 to be precise, was the MET electric tramway. In March 1938 trolleybus routes 521/ 621 ousted the trams; in November 1961 the wires came down for the trolleybuses when diesel buses were substituted. Meanwhile back on the railway front, the wires went up and the new Great Northern Electrics started operation in November 1976. What's next on the New Southgate transport merry-go-round? (R.J.Harley Coll.)

23. Station Road, New Southgate and the days of service 21 are numbered. Car 2108 projects a deceptive air of permanence, but on both sides of the street the new trolleybus traction standards are beginning to appear. (D.A.Thompson Coll.)

→

25. This card was posted on 14th June 1907 not long after New Southgate was connected to Wood Green and Finsbury Park by tramway. As one might expect, a number locals seem to have taken the day off to pose for the photographer. No doubt this view of one of the latest marvels of the electric age was enthusiastically sent to relatives and friends who had been denied this example of an up-to-date transport system, and were still stuck in the horse and cart era. (G.Bromberger Coll.)

26. Woodhouse Road, Finchley still presents a rural aspect as car 77 heads towards the terminus. The chap standing at the stop opposite won't have long to wait for his tram to Wood Green. (D.Jones Coll.)

27. A line of Edwardian terrace houses adds a firm middle class feel to Woodhouse Road. Supplying the public transport is car 113 which is displaying a route symbol featuring a red letter F on a white background with a blue edged circumference.   (J.Wills Coll.)

28. A Feltham car is just about to turn into Woodhouse Road from High Road, North Finchley. This area and the modernised 1930s tram layout is comprehensively described in *Barnet and Finchley Tramways*.   (D.Jones Coll.)

533.—EXTERIOR MIRRORS—FELTHAM CARS.

Notice to Motormen—Wood Green and Finchley Depots.

Collisions are being caused by some Motormen fixing the driving mirrors on Feltham cars, with string or other means, in an outward position.   Not only is damage caused but the record of the number of collisions is increased.

Motormen are reminded that these mirrors must be operated by hand and not fixed in an outward position.

WOOD GREEN DEPOT

29. The photographer is standing on Jolly Butchers Hill as he points his lens towards the entrances of Wood Green Depot. These car sheds were ready for electric traction from 1904, and until 1910 they also contained a repair works and paint shop for all the MET cars working the "northern lines". Subsequent to this date Hendon Car Works took over the task. This view shows the depot just prior to reconstruction work for the trolleybuses. (H.Nicol)

Wood Green 1912

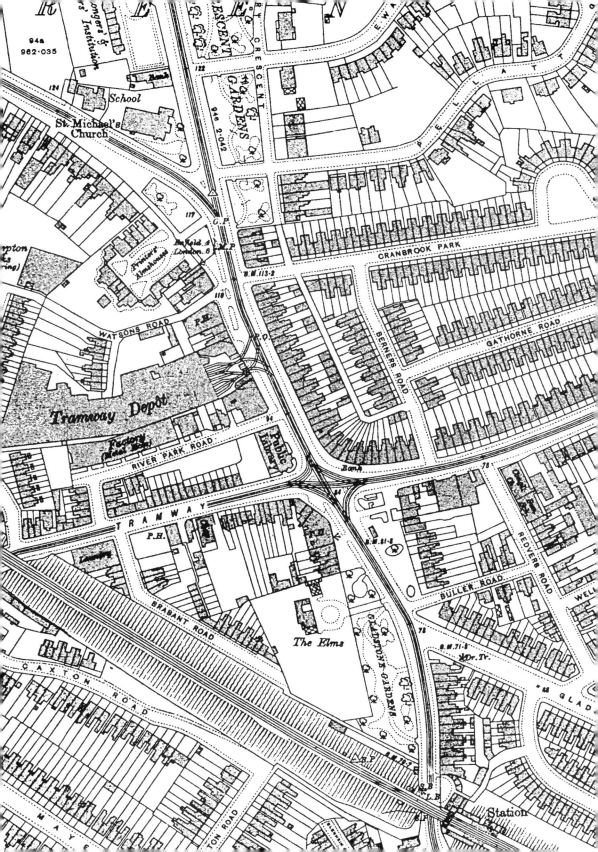

30. What a difference a couple of years makes! In 1937/8 the depot as seen here was enlarged and modified for trolleybuses. Car 2296 bowed out on the 51s on 6th March 1938. Symbolically a ladder reaches skywards to the new overhead wires for the replacing vehicles. Evidence of the original building can still be seen today. (B.J.Cross Coll.)

32. In the first few weeks of the London Transport regime, veteran car 193 pauses to have its image preserved for posterity before trundling away on service 51. Note the MET globe lamp on top of the gate pillar. (S.G.Jackman)

31. In happier days for the tramcar, car 329 is pictured in almost brand new condition as it occupies depot road 7. The shed between the tram and the retreating conductor is the resting place of the company tower wagon. (D.Jones Coll.)

33. Contrasting tramcar profiles are on display, as we look from type C/1 car 2294 to type E single decker, car 2303 and finally to a type UCC, Feltham car, next to the depot wall. (W.A.Camwell)

34. The fleet is assembled in advance of the big day when service begins. Depot staff are putting the finishing touches to cars 4 and 20 which possess stylish wrought iron railings on the top deck. Note the packing cases and the maintenance pits between the rails. (D.Jones Coll.)

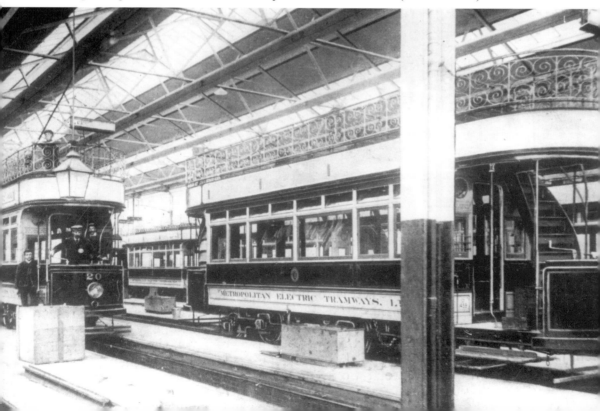

WOOD GREEN TO
ALEXANDRA PALACE EAST

35. At the foot of Jolly Butchers Hill was a "Grand Union" tramway junction connecting the High Road with tracks in Station Road and Lordship Lane. The motorman of car 156 applies the handbrake as he negotiates the points. This is a rare view, as type C/2 cars spent most of their working life in the north-western section of the MET. In the background is the spire of St.Michael's Church. (D.Jones Coll.)

36. Looking from the other direction to the previous view, we now observe Feltham car 2070 as it glides past the policeman on traffic duty. Another Feltham waits to proceed up Jolly Butchers Hill, whilst we catch a glimpse of yet another tram at the entrance to Lordship Lane. By the time this photo was taken in the mid-1930s the tracks east to west from Station Road to Lordship Lane had been cut. (D.Jones Coll.)

37. The photographer has set up his camera in Lordship Lane and we look across to car 147 which is having its trolley pole turned outside the public library. This view dates from before the First World War.   (R.Stevenson Coll.)

37	**WOOD GREEN — ALEXANDRA PALACE** Via Station Road Service interval 5—8 mins. (Wood Green—Wood Green Station only on Sundays). Journey time 9 mins. Through fare 1d.	Wood Green to Wood Green Station........	6 24	6 30	11 36	6 24	6 30	11 36	10 0	10 48
		Wood Green to Alexandra Palace..........	2 30	2 36	10 30	2 30	2 36	11 6	....	....
		Alexandra Palace to Wood Green............	2 41	2 47	10 40	2 41	2 47	11 16	....	....
		Wood Green Station to Wood Green........	6 30	6 36	11 42	6 30	6 36	11 42	10 6	10 54
39	**BRUCE GROVE—MUSWELL HILL** Via Lordship Lane, Wood Green, Turnpike Lane. Service interval 6—12 mins. Journey time, 22 mins. Through fare 4d. **WOOD GRN. (Wellington) — ALEXANDRA PAL.** Via Turnpike Lane, Muswell Hill. (Wood Green (Wellington)—Muswell Hill only on Sundays) Service interval (afternoons only), 7—9 minutes. Journey time, 13 minutes. Through fare 2d.	Bruce Grove to Wood Green Junction	6 39	6 45	1 2	6 39	6 45	1 21	7 42	12 9
		Wood Green Junction to Bruce Grove	6 27	6 33	12 50	6 27	6 33	1 9	7 30	11 57
		Bruce Grove to Muswell Hill	10 12	10 24	10 52	10 12	10 22	11 10	11 0	11 14
		Muswell Hill to Bruce Grove	9 28	10 1	11 16	9 57	10 6	11 34	10 36	11 44
		Muswell Hill to Wood Green (Wellington)	8 48	12 11	16	8 48	12 11	34	9 15	11 58
		Muswell Hill to Alexandra Palace	2 40	2 47	10 51	2 38	2 47	11 20	....	....
		Alexandra Palace to Wood Green (Wellington)	2 47	2 54	10 57	2 47	2 56	11 27	....	....
		Wood Green (Wellington) to Muswell Hill ..	7 53	8 0	11 5	7 53	8 0	11 24	9 0	11 48

38. Time has now advanced to the 1930s and we have crossed over into Station Road. Car 2314 waits to set off for Alexandra Palace East. Behind the tram is Wood Green tube station on the Piccadilly Line; this new transport facility opened in 1932. (D.Jones Coll.)

39. Station Road in 1933 and cars 137 and 150 have passed out of MET ownership into the hands of London Transport. In the background behind car 137 is the railway bridge carrying the Palace Gates branch which was opened by the Great Eastern Railway in October 1883 and closed by British Railways in January 1963 - yet another short sighted rail abandonment in the capital. (G.N.Southerden)

40. We now arrive at the Palace Gates branch bridge and we can clearly see why double deck operation was not permitted on Station Road. Today this site is easily identified by the prominent dip in the roadway. Posters advertise a number of sporting and variety events including a guest performance by Jack Payne and his BBC Band. The radio era (called "the wireless" in those days) had spawned a whole new chapter in popular entertainment. (C.F.Klapper)

41. A gloomy day in February 1938 matches the mood of local tram enthusiasts as car 2313 passes Caxton Road in the last week of operation. This vehicle was one of only two type Es to receive a Charlton overhaul. Therefore, as it was not fitted with conduit equipment, it was towed from Manor House, then through the Kingsway Subway into South London. (D.Jones Coll.)

42. By Wood Green Station we encounter car 142 which is working the short lived service from Alexandra Palace East to Bruce Grove. The regular route soon settled down to a Wood Green Station to Wood Green shuttle, with an extension to the Palace according to traffic demands and when the Park was open. The route from Wood Green LT Station to Wood Green LNER Station was the shortest on the entire London tramway system, with a journey time of just four minutes and fare of one old penny! (D.Jones Coll.)

43. On Buckingham Road opposite the station, car 2308 seems to have garnered some passengers for the return trip to Wood Green. In basic terms both Alexandra Palace services were hopelessly uneconomic and it is surprising that they lasted until 1938. (R.J.Harley Coll.)

44. Bridge Road, as the name suggests, carried the tramway over the Great Northern main line. One of the advantages of tramways over conventional "heavy" railways is the ability of the former to traverse tight curves and to tackle steep gradients. Car 2307 will have no problem on the sharp turn into Bedford Road. (C.Carter)

45. In the next two views we follow car 2309 as it negotiates the curve into Bedford Road surrounded by cyclists. The chap in the bowler hat demonstrates the correct way to cross tramlines without getting the front wheel caught in the groove. (B.J.Cross Coll.)

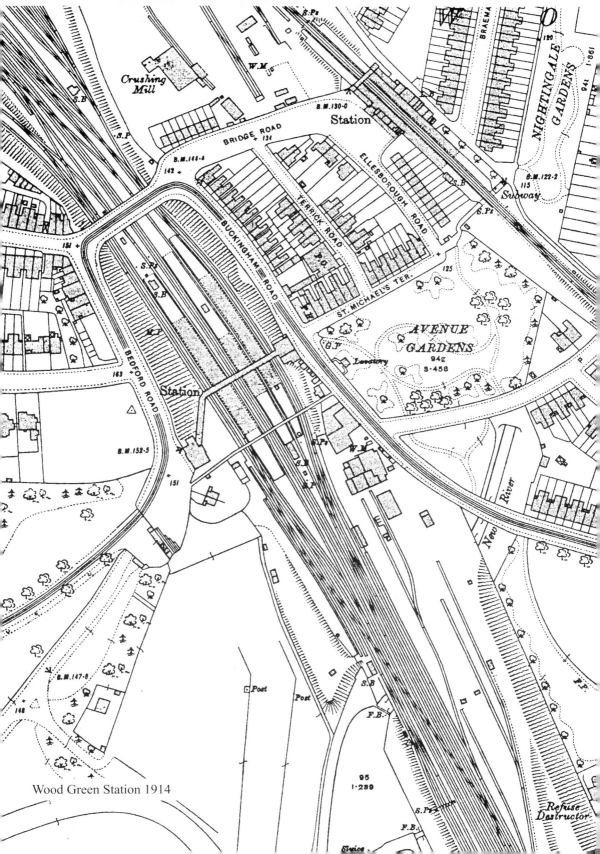

Wood Green Station 1914

46. A few moments later and car 2309 is about to reverse at the crossover by Wood Green Station. The poster on the rocker panel of the tram informs the general public of the imminent replacement of the Alexandra Palace routes by motor buses. (D.Jones Coll.)

No. 251.—POINTS—THE WELLINGTON, TURNPIKE LANE, SERVICES NOS. 34, 34 AND 51.

NOTICE TO CONDUCTORS—WOOD GREEN DEPOT.

When it is necessary for the staff on a car to move the points at The Wellington in Turnpike Lane, Conductors a reminded that in accordance with Rule 81, page 22 of Rule Book, the points must be replaced and at this point alwa left set for up cars to London.

47. When special events were taking place in the Palace or the Park, admission charges were levied. Tram travellers could buy combined tickets. In this early view, car 149 still lacks passengers as it halts at the Palace gates. (D.Jones Coll.)

48. Car 145 ascends to the terminus at Alexandra Palace East at the beginning of the tramway era. Most Londoners refer to the place affectionately as the "Ally Pally", and consequently the single deck trams serving the establishment were nicknamed "Ally Pally Bang Bangs". (D.Jones Coll.)

49. At the close of the tramway era, the trees still look the same and the tramcars haven't changed much either, the only noticeable alterations being the new LT red and cream livery and the repositioning of the headlamp from the roof to the dash. This picture conveys all the atmosphere of a leisurely tramway backwater a few days before abandonment. (D.W.K.Jones)

50. There was a scissors crossover at the terminus, but it seems from this photo that only the facing points were employed, the trailing connection appears to be disused. Car 2302 was the only member of type E not to have advertisement boards on the roof. Traffic on both tramway branches did pick up very marginally with the arrival of the world's first TV station in 1936, when the BBC started broadcasting from Alexandra Palace. It is also rumoured that unofficial outside broadcast camera trials went on with the assistance of motormen and conductors on the empty tramcars. (D.W.K.Jones)

51. This is the former car shed and generating station for the Alexandra Park Electric Railway. The fleet consisted of four cars and obviously the operators were not superstitious because public service began on Friday 13th May 1898. Unfortunately the omens were not good and the whole thing folded on 30th September 1899.   (D.Jones Coll.)

WOOD GREEN TO
THE WELLINGTON, TURNPIKE LANE

52. We now double back to Lordship Lane in time to witness the arrival of car 24 bearing the words SPECIAL CAR on the destination box. The date may well be around the summer of 1904 just after the route had opened. (J.Wills Coll.)

53. This is the first of four views at the same location in Wood Green High Road. Car 6 seems to be momentarily unattended as the motorman investigates something going on in the lower saloon. Note that in this scene of long ago you could stand in the highway or amble along the middle of the road without much likelihood of being knocked flat by the passing traffic! The buildings behind the tram would later be replaced by the Piccadilly Line station. (B.J.Cross Coll.)

54. Car 1592 in the middle of the picture is in the crimson lake and primrose livery of the London County Council; this paint style weathered eventually to a dull brown and cream. This vehicle is one of a number of E/1 cars which were on temporary loan to the MET. Either side of the LCC car are MET vehicles in their bright signal red and white livery. On the pavement, various members the tramway staff wait to replace colleagues coming off shift. For those potential passengers who don't want to stand in the sun, the shelter on the right offers a pleasant place to wait.   (D.Jones Coll.)

55. Car 306 is on the Euston Road to Palmers Green service and displays not only a route number, but also a standard LCC style three colour light indicator. The open top vehicle adjacent is working from Bruce Grove to Finsbury Park. Two LCC trams have just passed the depot on their ascent of Jolly Butchers Hill.   (D.Jones Coll.)

56. Our last view at the corner of Lordship Lane and the High Road was taken in 1932 and shows an MET Feltham and an LCC car from the 552-

601 series (fully described in *Hampstead and Highgate Tramways*). Motor bus competition is an ominous sign for the future. (D.Jones Coll.)

57. This rain-swept scene is of a type E passing under the railway bridge by Noel Park and Wood Green Station. The tram is probably on a journey from the depot to take up service on the Palace West branch. (C.F.Klapper)

58. MET car 313 passes the Round House at the corner of Mayes Road and Wood Green High Road. Note the stop sign and the street lamps attached to the traction standard on the left hand traffic island. This pole is also employed to carry the company's telephone wires. (J.Wills Coll.)

59. On the North Finchley to Finsbury Park service, C/1 type car 198 is seen on the opposite side of the road to the previous picture. This particular tram was built in 1908 by Brush of Loughborough and later modernised in 1929 with a fully enclosed top cover. It passed to LT in 1933 and was renumbered 2288; it was scrapped in 1938. The outfitters shop, Keevans, just behind the tram, had the contract to supply all school uniforms for the Hornsey Education Department.   (D.Jones Coll.)

60. Four wheel type D car 170 stands at The Wellington in Turnpike Lane in the late 1920s. This tram is working service 34 from Muswell Hill to Bruce Grove. Note the Thomas Tilling bus on route 21A.   (C.F.Klapper)

61. Car 147 (later LT 2313) seems to have been a favourite for photographers. There are quite a few people on board as the motorman poses beside his charge. As well as the passengers there appears to be a sack on the motorman's platform; it was quite usual for London trams to carry "light goods" i.e. flower baskets, large parcels etc. up front next to the driver. Of course this handy service ceased when the trams were replaced. (H.Nicol)

62. Car 131 waits, ready to work the short trip to Muswell Hill. Next to the Sunday Graphic poster, the black lettering on the foot of the rocker panel reads:

TYPE E LESSEES OF THE MIDDLESEX COUNTY COUNCIL.
(E.Masterman)

Turnpike Lane 1914

63. Two type D cars unload their passengers in the middle of the road. This was shortly to change, when the Piccadilly Line was extended northwards in 1932, new loading islands were built here with subways giving direct access to the new station. (D.Jones Coll.)

64. The islands completed, type C/1 car 2284, now in LT livery, pauses before continuing its journey to the foot of Muswell Hill. Today, the passenger shelter to the right of the picture is the only remaining evidence of this transport interchange. (D.W.K.Jones)

65. A few yards further along Turnpike Lane we observe cars 2281 and 2306 passing. The double deck tram was formerly MET car 236 of type G. These vehicles, with an overall height of just over 15 ft./ 4.6 metres, were able to squeeze under the railway bridge in Turnpike Lane. Note the plain front window on the top deck of car 2281, which did not carry the usual opening top light. (J.Pullen)

66. Looking towards Hornsey in 1905, we see track laying in progress. The roadway here was widened on the north side to accommodate the new electric trams. (D.Jones Coll.)

No. 230.—NEW SERVICE—ENFIELD AND BRUCE GROVE.

NOTICE TO STAFF—WOOD GREEN.

All concerned are hereby notified that with the introduction of the above service on Wednesday, 28th Februar 1934, a pull frog was fitted at Pole No. 6, on the up track, Jolly Butchers Hill, which must be operated by the conducto of cars proceeding into Lordship Lane.

67. The date is April 1908 and a late fall of snow brings out the local photographer. Car 178 has a good audience including many postmen from the nearby sorting office in Tottenham Lane. St.Mary's Church has since been replaced by a school, but some of the original boundary wall survives. (D.Jones Coll.)

68. By Middle Lane we see a well loaded type A car carrying passengers away from Muswell Hill, and a single decker en route to the Palace. The shops in this area were normally thronged with people, but on this occasion it appears unusually quiet.   (G.Bromberger Coll.)

39a BRUCE GROVE — WOOD GREEN — ENFIELD
Via Lordship Lane, Green Lanes, Aldermans Hill, Winchmore Hill.
Service Interval, Weekday rush hours only, 8 mins.
Journey time, 34 mins.   Through fare 6d.

Note : This service operates between Bruce Grove and Winchmore Hill only, on Monday to Friday evenings, and Saturday rush hours.

	MON. to FRI.		SATURDAY		SUNDAY	
	First	Last	First	Last	First	Last
Bruce Grove to Enfield .... morning	6 50	8 35	......	......	......	......
Bruce Grove to Enfield .... afternoon	5 13	7 8	......	......	......	......
Bruce Grove to Winchmore Hill .. morning	6 50	9 7	6 50	9 7	......	......
Bruce Grove to Winchmore Hill ..afternoon	4 18	10 53	1154	2 50	......	......
Enfield to Bruce Grove ....morning	7 27	8 31	......	......	......	......
Enfield to Bruce Grove ....afternoon	5 50	7 38	......	......	......	......
Winchmore Hill to Bruce Grove ....morning	7 35	8 39	7 19	9 34	......	......
Winchmore Hill to Bruce Grove ..afternoon	3 50	11 10	1223	2 24	......	......

Last car Weekdays, Wood Green to Bruce Grove 12.50.   Bruce Grove to Wood Green 1.2

Item No. 606.—Muswell Hill Route.

NOTICE TO MOTORMEN.

Complaint has been made that cars are not stopped at the corner of Church Lane, on journey to Muswell Hill but invariably stopped at the Parish Church, so that intending passengers from Church Lane are often left behind

Motormen are instructed to stop car at the proper stopping place, and Conductors to keep a sharp look out for would-be passengers.

69. Car 73 passes along Priory Road near Nightingale Lane.   (J.Wills Coll.)

70. At the corner of Linzee Road, car 147 halts to be photographed. The street names here are marked on a frosted section of glass at the top of the lamp standard. Note the wonderful collection of local "worthies" all trying to get into the act!   (D.Jones Coll.)

71. Car 79 is at the Muswell Hill terminus in this 1906 scene. The conductor is on the top deck, and having turned the trolley pole, he is just about to put it on the wire for the journey back to Finsbury Park. The single deck car has just come from the private track in Alexandra Park.   (D.Jones Coll.)

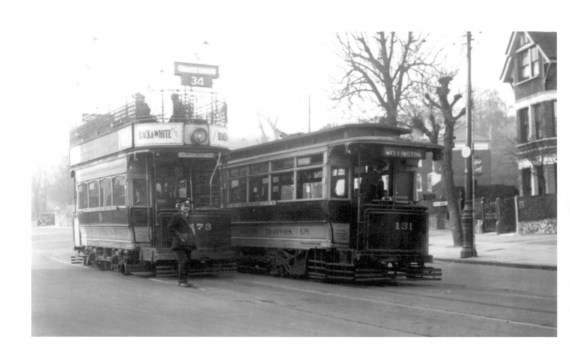

72. Facing in the opposite direction to the previous view, we note cars 173 and 131. The date is 26th December 1929 and Dr.Hugh Nicol, the well known tramway enthusiast, has obviously taken a break from the Christmas festivities to capture this scene on film. The traction standard on the right has a couple of bamboo poles for rewiring errant trolleys; note also the fare stage number 13. (H.Nicol)

74. Car 2303 is about to enter the reserved track leading up the hill to the Palace. This picture has a certain timeless quality, and unfortunately for the trams, the scene is passengerless as well. (D.W.K.Jones)

73. Here we see tracks being laid from Muswell Hill into the Palace grounds. While at this point they would be surfaced, shortly after entering the Park sleeper track would take over. (D.Jones Coll.)

75. In this mid-1930s view car 2302 leaves the Palace grounds and runs back on to paved track. The notice to the right lists the various entertainments on offer - licensed bars, concerts, dancing on the lawn - all rounded off with a tram ride home. (NTM Coll.)

77. The end of the line - this was built with direct access to the Palace via flights of steps - such was the provision for the crowds that were expected. Much of this work remains today, and the intrepid explorer can dive into the undergrowth and still see the tops of the brick pillars peering out from subsequent earthworks. (D.Jones Coll.)

76. Further up the hill we have a good view of the ballasted sleeper track with a footpath alongside. The present day roadway follows the course of this tramway. (B.Y.Williams)

78. A last look at the Palace reveals car 133 with its trolley turned ready for the descent to Turnpike Lane. In winter some of the tram crews used to pull faces at the firemen and engine drivers in the adjacent railway station. The response of the train staff was to chuck pieces of coal at the cheeky individuals on the tram side. The fuel was subsequently gathered up to light a fire at the tram terminus. The trip to the Wellington and back was then done in double quick time, so that frozen motormen and conductors could be assured of a few minutes thawing out in front of the fire. (C.F.Klapper)

GREEN LANES, HARRINGAY TO MANOR HOUSE

79. Heavy rains in July 1907 brought flooding to Green Lanes, where car 80 wades through the water to Wood Green. This card was published under the title "Harringay's annual excursion to the seaside!" (D.Jones Coll.)

80. Working to Finsbury Park, type B car 23 attempts to edge past a heavily loaded horse drawn wagon in this busy shopping area. As today, deliveries had to go ahead to commercial premises, thus presenting an inconvenience for passing traffic. (D.Jones Coll.)

81. Car 207 passes the Coliseum Picture Palace, which was situated on the corner of St.Ann's Road, close to the Salisbury public house. In the background an LCC car heads northwards on service 71. (D.A.Thompson Coll.)

82. Type D car 173 has just passed below the bridge of the Tottenham and Hampstead Junction Railway at Harringay Park, Green Lanes Station. The station was opened as Green Lanes on 1st June 1880. Just beyond the bridge was Harringay Stadium, a most popular venue for speedway and greyhound racing. Many thousands of people were carried to and from the races by tram. (D.Jones Coll.)

83. Feltham car 354 waits at the Manor House stop before descending the hill towards Harringay Park Station. Open windows and platform doors would suggest that North Londoners are enjoying a fine summer's day. This view is opposite the entrance to the old MET yard, where horse tram tracks exist to this day. A couple of single deck trams were stored in this yard nightly, owing to there being no room available at Wood Green Depot.   (D.Jones Coll.)

84. Making the right turn from Green Lanes is car 2058. It will shortly pause at the change pit in Seven Sisters Road, where the conductor will stow the trolley pole and the car will pick up a conduit plough for the further journey towards the West End and the Tottenham Court Road terminus. Note the stylish 1930s signpost in the middle of the carriageway. (J.Pullen)

Manor House 1915

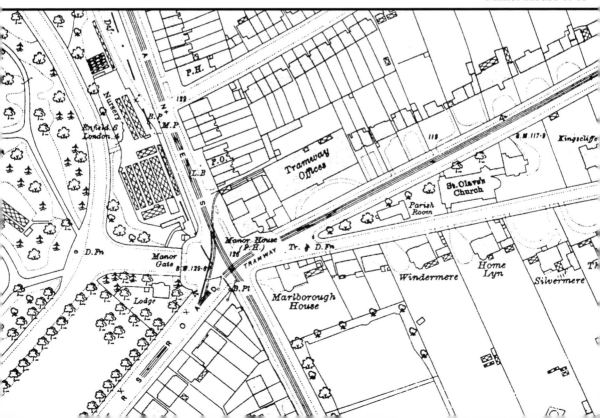

85. Green Lanes, on the south side of Manor House, also possessed a change pit. Here the conductor of car 2236 ties up the trolley rope, having already turned the pole for the return journey, as the attendant forks the plough under the car. This picture dates from 6th March to 30th April 1938, as this was the period that ex-MET cars worked the route. Tram route 41 became trolleybus route 641 and in 1961, electric traction gave way to diesel bus route 141. (R.J.Harley Coll.)

86. We remain at the same location, but time has now advanced to 1941. E/1 car 1262 is one of eight previously withdrawn trams that were returned to service from Hampstead Depot as a wartime emergency measure. This tram originally worked a shuttle - Balls Pond to Bloomsbury and Archway to Bloomsbury. The section of track between Balls Pond Road and Manor House was damaged by bombing in September 1940, and by the time the service to Manor House was restored in April 1941, ex-Leyton E/3s had been drafted into Holloway to replace six of the old E/1s. Cars 1107 and 1262 were the only two left in service that reached Manor House. Various wartime changes to car 1262 are the early type of headlamp mask, and the white paint added to the collision fenders, platform steps and to the main staircase. Note the exhortation from the Metropolitan Water Board to use less of their product. (D.W.K.Jones)

87. On the other side of the junction towards Tottenham, stands the main office of the Metropolitan Electric Tramways, which can be seen here as the ivy clad building on the left. The MET inscription can still be seen today above the main doorway; a siding from Green Lanes into an adjacent yard is also visible at the time of writing. The loading islands with the classic UndergrounD bulls eye symbol were built here when the Piccadilly tube was extended in 1932. Car 2219, one of the few type H cars to have upholstered seats on the top deck, unloads directly on to the island where passengers can transfer to the tube without having to cross the road. (A.B.Cross)

88. Type A car 118, equipped with a plough carrier to work over LCC lines, is caught on camera at Manor House on a rush hour special service 27. This car is believed to be one of the vehicles equipped with a searchlight during the First World War. Such trams were stationed at "strategic" points on the MET system; they were manned by military personnel and their main task was to illuminate German bombers and Zeppelin airships. The excitement must have been too much for car 118, because shortly after this view was taken, it overturned at Enfield on 11th December 1929. To compound the offence, it had just been given a new top cover! It did not survive long enough to receive an LT number. (H.Nicol)

89. The inspector on the extreme left seems to be oblivious to the fact that trams are hurtling past a few inches behind him! The motorman of car 113 seems to take all this in his stride as he waits seemingly unconcerned in a line of cars at Seven Sisters Road change pit. In the heyday of the tramcar this was one of the favourite spots where a dedicated enthusiast could watch the trams go by. (H.Nicol)

MORE PICTURES OF MANOR HOUSE AND FINSBURY PARK ARE CONTAINED IN *STAMFORD HILL TRAMWAYS* MIDDLETON PRESS

90. Any problems on the tramway system would cause a long hold up as trams could not so easily be diverted around a blockage. Here we see car 2051 full of smoke probably as a result of an electrical fault. In attendance is Conductor Reynolds and the fire brigade who have succeeded in blocking the remaining part of the roadway. A Leyland belonging to the City Coach Company passes in the opposite direct. It is heading out of the smoke towards the holiday beaches of Southend-on-Sea, and yet more trams!   (D.W.K.Jones)

79 WALTHAM X. — FINSBURY PK. — SMITHFIELD Via Ponders End, Edmonton, Bruce Grove, Tottenham, Seven Sisters Rd., Manor House, Finsbury Pk., Holloway, Highbury. Upper St., Angel. St. John St. Service interval, Weekdays 6-8 mins. Journey time, 73 mins. Through fare 1/1. On Sundays this service operates between Enfield and Smithfield, via Southbury Rd., Ponders End, then as Weekday route. Service interval, Sundays, 6-8 minutes. Journey time, 62 minutes. Through fare 11d.									
Waltham Cross to Edmonton Town Hall	4 56	5 26	1152	4 56	5 26	1220	......	......	..
Waltham Cross to Smithfield	4 56	5 26	1020	4 56	5 26	1050	......	......	..
Waltham Cross to Finsbury Park	4 56	5 26	1137	4 56	5 26	1144	......	......	..
Waltham Cross to Edmonton depot	4 56	5 26	1224	4 56	5 26	1230	......	......	..
Smithfield to Waltham Cross	5 50	6 0	1112	5 50	6 0	1116	9 35	1138	..
Smithfield to Edmonton depot	5 50	6 0	1136	5 50	6 0	12 5	......	......	..
Edmonton depot to Waltham Cross	4 38	5 7	12 7	4 38	5 7	1211	......	......	..
Edmonton depot to Finsbury Park	4 19	4 33	1154	4 19	4 33	12 0	8 0	12 4	..
Edmonton depot to Smithfield	4 49	5 5	1037	4 49	5 5	11 7	8 42	1044	..
Enfield to Smithfield	......	......	......	......	......	......	8 31	1033	..
Enfield to Finsbury Park	......	......	......	......	......	......	8 0	1153	..
Enfield to Edmonton depot	......	......	......	......	......	......	8 0	1156	..
Smithfield to Enfield	......	......	......	......	......	......	9 35	1054	..
Edmonton depot to Enfield	......	......	......	......	......	......	7 47	1144	..

91. Car 223 was one of four type G cars allocated to Edmonton Depot to work service 79. It has just come under the control of the London Passenger Transport Board who will renumber much of the fleet. Only the ex-LCC cars retained their original numbers en masse. Many of the older cars will not be so lucky and they will make the one way journey to the breakers yard. The car shown here will live on for another five years.   (M.J.O'Connor)

92. The conductor of car 1269 has already put the trolley on the wire. Soon the driver will operate the changeover switch and the car will move off drawing power from the overhead. In the foreground can be seen the plough fork used by the attendant to help guide the plough into the carrier under London bound tramcars. This particular tram was one of four E/1s that were fitted with higher powered motors from ex-MET trams. Unfortunately, the bodies did not prove strong enough to stand up to the higher speeds. Car 1269 was the last tram of all to depart from Wood Green and its final run down Lordship Lane must have been one of the fastest rides ever known on an E/1 car! Service 53 is covered largely by the present day 253 bus, having had a trolleybus interlude as route 653 from 1939 to 1961. (D.Jones Coll.)

93. We look towards Manor House as this Feltham car on service 29 has just picked up its plough. (J.Pullen)

FINSBURY PARK TO NAGS HEAD

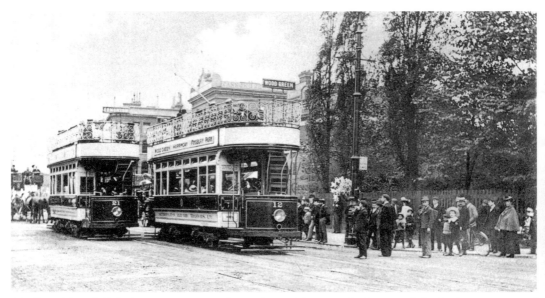

94. Cars 21 and 12 belong to type B and are pictured here at Finsbury Park in the late summer of 1904 after the opening of the service to Edmonton. Car 12 was withdrawn in 1926 to serve in the works fleet, its number was then allocated to a new H type car. Car 21 was withdrawn from service in 1931 when the Feltham cars were delivered.   (B.J.Cross Coll.)

95. Crowds gather to look at the new electric cars, and we observe cars 12 and 13 working the service to Wood Green.   (D.Jones Coll.)

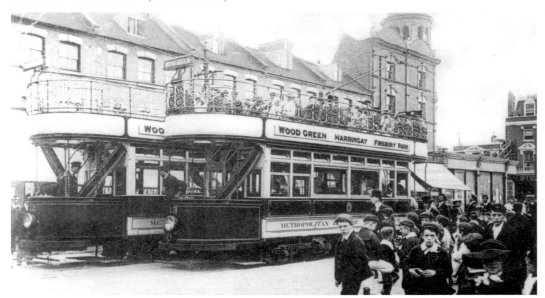

96. A tale of two B types, as the rivals line up at Finsbury Park. We encounter car 21 again and note the elegant lines of the environmentally friendly tramcar with its wrought iron tracery around the top deck. The London General Omnibus Company vehicle is of a type which performed sterling service during the First World War, when buses were called upon to transport troops to the front. (D.Jones Coll.)

97. Service 21 has given way to the 521 trolleybus which here demonstrates its flexibility in being able to pull into the kerbside at stops. Passengers wanting to board the 53 tramcar will have to walk out into the roadway. Because the trams were officially on their way out, LT was not inclined to install tramway loading islands such as the MET had supplied at Turnpike Lane and Manor House. This 1938 view also shows the three track layout laid by the LCC so that terminating cars did not hold up those on through services. (C.F.Klapper)

98. Here we see a group of horse cars standing at the Finsbury Park terminus. The two arched doorways of the depot are clearly visible, as is the complex track layout for reversing cars. (D.Jones Coll.)

99. Service 79 was still being operated by unscreened cars of type H on 26th July 1938. This tram route was replaced by the 679 trolleybus on 16th October 1938. The bridge in the background carries the tracks to Finsbury Park Station which was opened on 1st July 1861. (H.B.Priestley)

100. At the LCC style request stop by Isledon Road we note one of the new MET Feltham cars introduced in 1931 on service 21. They were a vast improvement over their predecessors, featuring such luxuries as platform doors, heaters and deep sprung seats in both saloons. The driver was rewarded with a separate cabin equipped with a seat. A car of type H can be seen alongside on service 59 to Edmonton Town Hall.
(M.J.O'Connor)

101. Here we see MET car 223 in its original open top state. It presents a contrast with the covered top LCC cars. All vehicles are drawing their power from the underground conduit system.   (J.Wills Coll.)

102. Viewed from the upper deck of a tram, we encounter ex-MET car 311 now masquerading as LT car 2243 in the Seven Sisters Road. This tram was the last type H car to be broken up; plans were made by the Light Railway Transport League to preserve it, but lack of a suitable storage site ended the project. Passengers are alighting at the stop close to Hornsey Road. Despite a green light the motorist will have to wait until the road is clear before passing the tram on the nearside.
(D.Jones Coll.)

103. A turn of the century scene in Seven Sisters Road, Holloway, depicts a North Metropolitan horse car on the Manor House to Moorgate service. (D.Jones Coll.)

104. At the Nags Head tramway junction, MET car 261 approaches the policeman on point duty. On the left an LCC car bound for Tottenham on service 27 swings past a horse drawn van. Although the conduit system was expensive to maintain, the skyline looks neater without all the overhead associated with complicated crossing layouts. (D.A.Thompson Coll.)

105. Overhead wires did appear later outside the Nags Head when trolleybuses were all the vogue and this location later became London's busiest trolleybus junction. Here car 2179 turns from Seven Sisters Road into Holloway Road. This tram is heading towards Smithfield having come from Waltham Cross in Hertfordshire and taking a journey time of an hour and a quarter.   (D.W.K.Jones)

106. The crossroads outside the Nags Head was always busy, even early in the electric tramway era. In this classic study, LCC car 1059 passes a taxi cab whilst the local PC keeps a wary eye out for traffic coming south along the Holloway Road. Car 1059 is about to cross into Parkhurst Road on a short working to Camden Town Station (North London Railway).   (D.Jones Coll.)

ROLLING STOCK

Alexandra Park Electric Railway

This was an ill fated venture whose short existence covered around 16 months in the years 1898-99. It was constructed by the Wandruszka Elektrizitaetsgesellschaft (electric company) of Berlin. The four single deck cars were likewise of German origin having been constructed in Hamburg at the Falkenried establishment of the local tramways. The fleet ran on a route of just over a quarter of a mile in length. This went from the Park gates to what was known later as the MET's Alexandra Palace East terminus. This little tramway's claim to fame was that it provided the first true electric tramway in London, predating the London United Tramways who opened for business in April 1901.

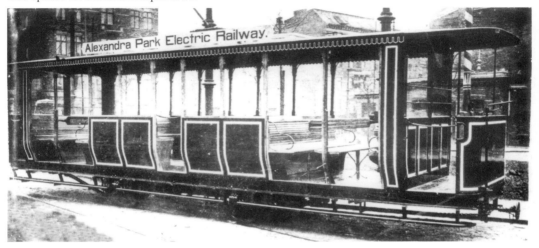

107. One of the four standard gauge vehicles which inaugurated the Alexandra Park Electric Railway is seen at the works in Hamburg. Each tram rode on a 6ft./1829mm wheelbase single truck, and the livery was probably dark green. After closure the fleet was acquired by the Great Grimsby Tramway Company and all the cars were converted to double deckers and mounted on Brill 21E trucks. (D.Jones Coll.)

MET Type E

These trams operated the Alexandra Palace services. Readers are reminded that MET types B, G and H are described in *Stamford Hill Tramways*; types C, C/1, C/2, and the experimental tramcars 318, 319, 320, 330 and 331 are described in *Barnet and Finchley Tramways*.

Type E cars 131-150.

These were single deck vehicles built in 1905 by Brush of Loughborough. They rode on Brush radial trucks of 8ft. 6ins./2591mm wheelbase. As originally constructed the lower saloon was divided into smoking and non-smoking saloons which were separated by a bulkhead and sliding doors. The two platform bulkheads also had double sliding doors. The internal partition of each car was rendered superfluous because the Metropolitan Police refused to countenance smoking on these single deckers, and the internal bulkheads were later removed. Spencer mechanical track brakes were used for the gradients in the Park and the Lycett and Conaty axle boxes were later replaced with Warner radial gear. Cars 132, 134, 137, 139, 140, 142, 146 and 150 were all later fitted with Spencer-Dawson hydraulic oil brakes. Around 1914 several E type cars were surplus to requirements and they were seconded to the works fleet to act as breakdown cars and ticket vans. Fifteen cars passed into LT ownership and were renumbered 2302-2316. Eleven cars were in service when the Alexandra Palace routes closed in 1938, and all the remaining E type vehicles were then sent for scrap.

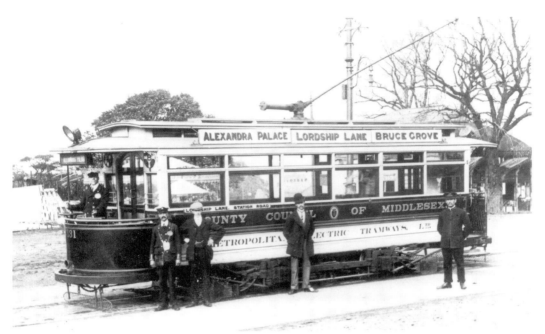

108. Car 131, the first of type E, is pictured in original condition at Alexandra Palace. Note the Wilson & Bennett wire-mesh lifeguards which were soon replaced by the standard Hudson & Bowring wooden slat variety. The early type trolley base was also later substituted by a conventional dwarf base. (D.Jones Coll.)

109. From the Alexandra Palace to the Crystal Palace! Cars 145 and 150 were loaned to the South Metropolitan Electric Tramways Company in August 1920. Here car 145 is seen in Penge Depot yard. Note that the words County Council of Middlesex have been painted out on the waist panel. Since the car was working the Robin Hood to Crystal Palace shuttle service in Kent, the Middlesex title was inappropriate. Car 145 also turned out on the Sutton to Wallington shuttle in Surrey! Both trams did not live up to expectations and were returned to the MET in 1925. (W.Gratwicke)

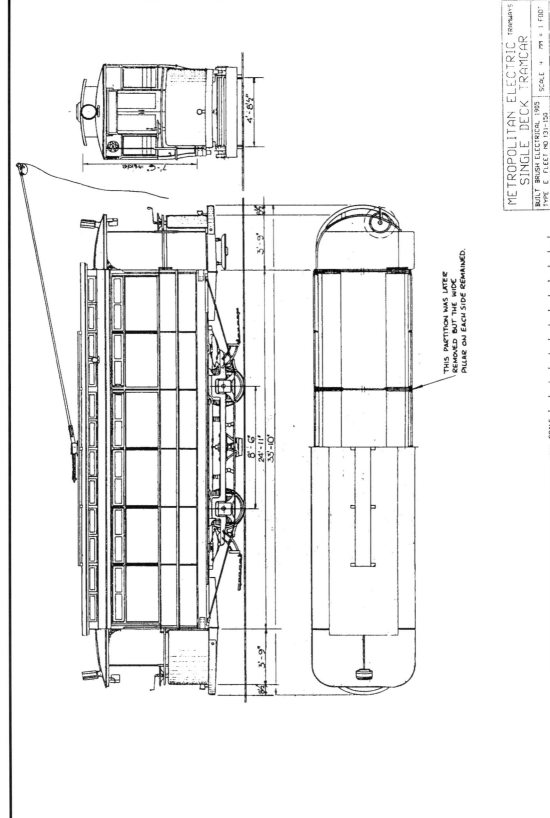

THIS PARTITION WAS LATER
REMOVED BUT THE WIDE
PILLAR ON EACH SIDE REMAINED.

7'-5" inside

4'-8½"

3'-9"

8'-6"
24'-11"
35'-10"

3'-9"

METROPOLITAN ELECTRIC TRAMWAYS
SINGLE DECK TRAMCAR

BUILT BRUSH ELECTRICAL 1905 | SCALE 4 MM = 1 FOOT
TYPE E FLEET NO 131-150

DRAWING No TC 10

SCALE
FEET 0 1 2 3 4 5 6 7 8 9 10 11 12

AVAILABLE FROM :- TERRY RUSSELL, "CHACESIDE", ST LEONARDS PARK, HORSHAM, W. SUSSEX. RH13 6EG.
SEND 3 FIRST CLASS STAMPS FOR COMPLETE LIST OF PUBLIC TRANSPORT DRAWINGS.

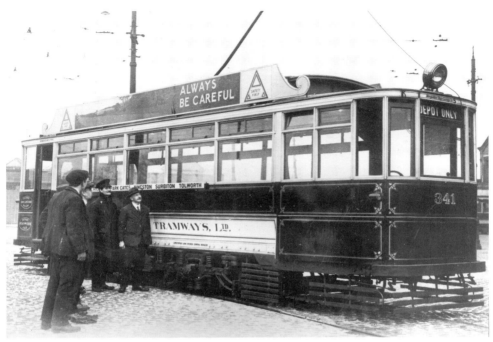

110. Car 132 was damaged in an accident on Easter Monday 1920 and the opportunity was taken to rebuild it as a one man operated tram. The car was sold in 1922 to the London United Tramways where it was renumbered 341, and is described in more detail in *Kingston and Wimbledon Tramways*. It is seen here at Fulwell Depot.   (LUT)

111. Cars 135, 136, 143 and 144 were sold in 1907 to Auckland in New Zealand. The red livery of this ex-MET car was retained although the car was renumbered 66.
(J.Hambley Coll.)

112. Auckland 66 again, this time it is mounted on equal wheel bogies; other alterations include a smoking saloon and driver's windscreens. (D.Jones Coll.)

113. This view presents an interesting contrast with the Auckland car. Note the 1920s livery style and the roof mounted advertising boards - in this case extolling the virtues of LIPTON'S TEA (white letters on dark green background). (MET)

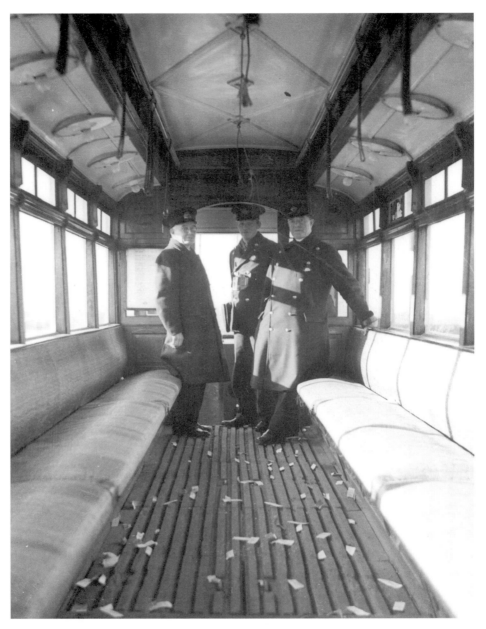

114. A 1938 view of the interior shows the bench seats and three members of staff - motorman, conductor and inspector. The litter on the floor consists mainly of discarded tickets, which of course would now fetch premium prices for today's collectors! Also to be noted is the clerestory roof and the straps for any standing passengers who had trouble keeping their balance on the gallop down the hill. (D.W.K.Jones)

115. Outside Wood Green LNER Station we are treated to an end view of car 2309, to be precise this is the no.2 end as the small figure to the right of the indicator box shows. To the left of the box is a standard LT notice stating amongst other things: NO SMOKING ALLOWED ON THE LOWER DECK. No doubt this rather odd warning for a single deck car meant that nicotine addicts were obliged to sit on the roof and keep the trolley pole company!
(B.J.Cross Coll.)

116. Car 2315, former MET car 149, is seen at Wood Green Depot in final London Transport condition. (W.A.Camwell)

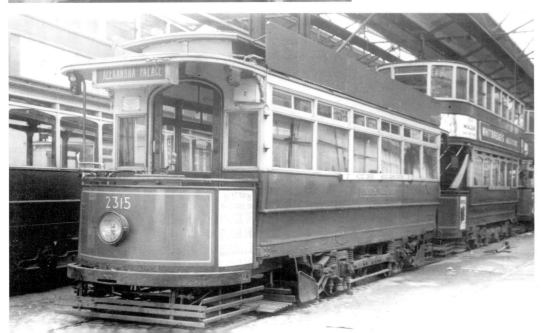

FINALE

117. The year 1933 saw the first appearance of the ex-Walthamstow cars in the Enfield area. These cars were probably the fastest in the fleet and also unfortunately the noisiest, in particular the 2042-2053 batch, so much so that conversations in the lower saloon were normally drowned by the whine of the motors and gears. Car 2057 waits at Enfield to whisk away its passengers! (G.N.Southerden)

118. As well as the ex-Walthamstow trams, the Feltham cars were also destined to be transferred south of the river to Telford Avenue, Streatham Depot. Not long before its departure, this Feltham leaves Wood Green Depot. Note that the area is already festooned with trolleybus wires. (R.J.Harley Coll.)

709.—(1) ABANDONMENT OF TRAM ROUTES 37 AND 39. (2) DIVERSION OF ROUTE 51 TO WOOD GREEN STATION (PICCADILLY LINE).

Notice to Inspectors and Conductors—Holloway, Hackney, Finchley and Wood Green Depots.

On Wednesday, 23rd February, 1938, the following alterations to services will take place :—

(a) Route 37 ... ... Alexandra Palace East and Wood Green Station (Piccadilly Line) will be abandoned and the road worked by Central Bus Route No. 241.

(b) Route 39 ... ... Alexandra Palace West and Bruce Grove Station will be abandoned and the road between Muswell Hill and Turnpike Lane Station worked by Central Bus Route No. 144, 144a and 144b.

(c) Route 51 ... ... Muswell Hill and Aldersgate will operate between Wood Green Station, Piccadilly Line, and Aldersgate.

In order to provide for the withdrawal of direct workman facilities via Turnpike Lane Station, the following 2d workman transfer journeys will be introduced. These transfer tickets will be issuable from tram to bus and vice versa.

Change at Turnpike Lane Station. ⎫ To be issued on trams arriving at Turnpike Lane Station up to 7.51 a.m.,
Muswell Hill and Manor House. ⎬ and accepted on trams leaving Turnpike Lane Station for Manor
Myddleton Road and Lordship Park. ⎭ House up to 7.55 a.m., and for Lordship Park up to 7.34 a.m.

Specimens of revised farebill for Route 51 and of revised 2d. workman tickets will be exhibited in the Depot, together th specimens of bus tickets to be accepted. The procedure for cancellation of bus tickets will be the same as is the esent practice on trams.

The transfer sections are printed above a double line and conductors accepting tickets for cancellation will, on the m on the outward journey, cancel below double line on same edge as punch hole, and on the tram on the return arney, cancel above double line opposite punch hole.

Holloway conductors will note that on the 29, 39a, 41, 2d. workman ticket certain transfers appear for journeys ange at Wood Green Station and Nags Head. These sections are provided for later contingencies and must not be ed until further notice.

119. Trolleybus route 645 arrived at North Finchley in August 1936, and for a few months operated alongside tram route 21. However, the rail bound vehicles would soon be ousted from this spot as the conversion programme swept across North London. (D.Jones Coll.)

120. The final act - here on the scrap sidings behind Walthamstow Depot the last members of the MET type E meet their fate. According to the notebooks of local enthusiast, David Bayes, car 2302 in the foreground perished on 28th February 1938. Thus the "Ally Pally Bang Bangs" finally fizzled out. (D.Jones Coll.)

MP Middleton Press

Easebourne Lane, Midhurst, West Sussex. GU29 9AZ Tel: 01730 813169 Fax: 01730 812601
... WRITE OR PHONE FOR OUR LATEST LIST ...

BRANCH LINES
Branch Line to Allhallows
Branch Lines to Alton
Branch Lines around Ascot
Branch Line to Ashburton
Branch Lines around Bodmin
Branch Line to Bude
Branch Lines around Canterbury
Branch Line to Cheddar
Branch Lines to East Grinstead
Branch Lines to Effingham Junction
Branch Line to Fairford
Branch Line to Hawkhurst
Branch Line to Hayling
Branch Line to Horsham
Branch Line to Ilfracombe
Branch Lines to Longmoor
Branch Line to Lyme Regis
Branch Line to Lynton
Branch Lines around Midhurst
Branch Line to Minehead
Branch Lines to Newport (IOW)
Branch Line to Padstow
Branch Lines around Plymouth
Branch Lines around Portmadoc 1923-46
Branch Lines around Porthmadog 1954-94
Branch Lines to Seaton & Sidmouth
Branch Line to Selsey
Branch Lines around Sheerness
Branch Line to Southwold
Branch Line to Swanage
Branch Line to Tenterden
Branch Lines to Torrington
Branch Line to Upwell
Branch Lines around Wimborne
Branch Lines around Wisbech

SOUTH COAST RAILWAYS
Ashford to Dover
Brighton to Eastbourne
Chichester to Portsmouth
Dover to Ramsgate
Portsmouth to Southampton
Ryde to Ventnor
Worthing to Chichester

SOUTHERN MAIN LINES
Bromley South to Rochester
Charing Cross to Orpington
Crawley to Littlehampton
Dartford to Sittingbourne
East Croydon to Three Bridges
Epsom to Horsham
Exeter to Barnstaple
Exeter to Tavistock
Faversham to Dover
Haywards Heath to Seaford
London Bridge to East Croydon
Orpington to Tonbridge
Sittingbourne to Ramsgate
Swanley to Ashford
Tavistock to Plymouth
Victoria to Bromley South
Waterloo to Windsor

Woking to Portsmouth
Woking to Southampton
Yeovil to Exeter

COUNTRY RAILWAY ROUTES
Bath to Evercreech Junction
Bournemouth to Evercreech Jn.
Burnham to Evercreech Junction
Croydon to East Grinstead
East Kent Light Railway
Fareham to Salisbury
Frome to Bristol
Guildford to Redhill
Porthmadog to Blaenau
Reading to Basingstoke
Reading to Guildford
Redhill to Ashford
Salisbury to Westbury
Strood to Paddock Wood
Taunton to Barnstaple
Westbury to Bath
Woking to Alton
Yeovil to Dorchester

GREAT RAILWAY ERAS
Ashford from Steam to Eurostar
Festiniog in the Fifties
Festiniog in the Sixties

LONDON SUBURBAN RAILWAYS
Caterham and Tattenham Corner
Clapham Jn. to Beckenham Jn.
Crystal Palace and Catford Loop
East London Line
Finsbury Park to Alexandra Palace
Holborn Viaduct to Lewisham
Lines around Wimbledon
London Bridge to Addiscombe
Mitcham Junction Lines
North London Line
South London Line
West Croydon to Epsom
West London Line
Willesden Junction to Richmond
Wimbledon to Epsom

STEAM PHOTOGRAPHERS
O.J.Morris's Southern Railways 1919-59

STEAMING THROUGH
Steaming through Cornwall
Steaming through East Sussex
Steaming through the Isle of Wight
Steaming through Kent
Steaming through West Hants
Steaming through West Sussex

TRAMWAY CLASSICS
Aldgate & Stepney Tramways
Barnet & Finchley Tramways
Bath Tramways
Bournemouth & Poole Tramways
Brighton's Tramways
Bristol's Tramways

Camberwell & W.Norwood Tramways
Croydon's Tramways
Clapham & Streatham Tramways
Dover's Tramways
East Ham & West Ham Tramways
Eltham & Woolwich Tramways
Embankment & Waterloo Tramways
Enfield & Wood Green Tramways
Exeter & Taunton Tramways
Gosport & Horndean Tramways
Greenwich & Dartford Tramways
Hampstead & Highgate Tramways
Hastings Tramways
Holborn & Finsbury Tramways
Ilford & Barking Tramways
Kingston & Wimbledon Tramways
Lewisham & Catford Tramways
Liverpool Tramways 1. Eastern Routes
Maidstone & Chatham Tramways
North Kent Tramways
Portsmouth's Tramways
Reading Tramways
Seaton & Eastbourne Tramways
Southampton Tramways
Southend-on-sea Tramways
Southwark & Deptford Tramways
Stamford Hill Tramways
Thanet's Tramways
Victoria & Lambeth Tramways
Walthamstow & Leyton Tramways
Wandsworth & Battersea Tramways

TROLLEYBUS CLASSICS
Croydon's Trolleybuses
Hastings Trolleybuses
Maidstone Trolleybuses
Reading Trolleybuses
Woolwich & Dartford Trolleybuses

WATERWAY ALBUMS
Hampshire Waterways
Kent and East Sussex Waterways
London's Lost Route to the Sea
London to Portsmouth Waterway
Surrey Waterways

MILITARY BOOKS
Battle over Portsmouth
Battle over Sussex 1940
Blitz over Sussex 1941-42
Bombers over Sussex 1943-45
Bognor at War
Military Defence of West Sussex
Secret Sussex Resistance

OTHER BOOKS
Brickmaking in Sussex
Garraway Father & Son
Index to all Stations
Industrial Railways of the South East
London Chatham & Dover Railway

SOUTHERN RAILWAY VIDEO
War on the Line